Our planet needs help. To try t
a few trees is like putting a ban
limb. *Much* more is needed.

More than anything else, the savagery of the marauder
needs to be tamed. Mass anger needs softening by a new
respect for the power of kindness and love. Human consciousness must be uplifted. If enough people worked to
change themselves, instead of telling other people how *not*
to live, our "green and fertile earth" might become once
again the paradise we all know it could be.

This book is my sincere attempt to inspire people everywhere—to inspire *you,* friend—to make your life what,
deep in your heart, you know it might be, if only you'd
stop telling yourself, "Oh, but I could never do *that.*"

J. Donald Walters

Do It NOW!

J. Donald Walters

CRYSTAL
CLARITY

Cover Illustration: Bella Bingham
Design: Crystal Clarity Design
Art Direction: Christine Schuppe

International Standard Book Number: 1-565-89-731-5
Printed in the United States of America
Printed on recycled paper
10 9 8 7 6 5 4 3 2 1

CRYSTAL

CLARITY

14618 Tyler Foote Road
Nevada City CA 95959
1-800-424-1055

This book may be used in several ways. It was intended, to begin with, as a diary of helpful thoughts for the 366 days of the year (including leap year). I became increasingly aware while working on it, however, that this was also a book to be read at random. I realized that you, the reader, would find certain of the sayings more meaningful than others, regardless of their placement in the calendar year. Thus, you might prefer to ignore the sequence. I have there-fore minimized the visual impact of the dates. You may find the numbering helpful as it stands, however, in case you want to locate again some particular saying, or to recommend one to a friend. You may also like to make use of the dating system to find thoughts for people's birthdays.

I hasten to add that I have followed no arcane system in placing the sayings. If what appears for your birthday happens to suit you, I may blushingly remark, "Well, of course, one *tries*." But if it misses the mark altogether, please just accept it as the luck of the draw. Or, alternatively, you might praise my tactfulness in preserving your secret by seeming to describe someone else altogether.

Only three of the sayings have been placed deliberately: February 14 (Valentine's Day), July 4 (Independence Day), and December 25 (Christmas), since these dates (unlike Easter, Thanksgiving, etc.) are fixed in our calendar. Should you be a monk or a nun in a monastery, or the native of another country, or be a non-Christian, it won't matter at all. The sayings are universal anyway.

My recommendation is that, once you've skimmed about at leisure, you begin following the sayings sequentially through the year and practicing their suggestions. For my idea has been to help you grow with the aid of something specific to do every day. Year by year, as you continue using this book, you'll find it serving you also as a measure of your mental and spiritual progress.

The sayings themselves evolved out of my life experiences: out of many years of testing, of trial and error, of sorrow (sometimes), and of joyful discovery (always).

1 Demolish difficulties from a higher level of consciousness. Gaze upward more often; center your awareness between the eyebrows (the seat of will power). Throughout the day, walk lightly, sit lightly. Smile upward more often, as if at the sky.

2 Smile with your eyes, not only with your lips.

3 When conversing with others face to face, communicate also with the eyes. When you express yourself only in words, you reduce your communication by half.

4 Watch your reactions when people or circumstances threaten your tranquillity. How you react is *your* choice and no one else's. Let no one force a reaction from you that would diminish your own peace of mind.

5 When conversing, talk *with* people, not *at* them.

6 Laugh more from the heart than from the intellect.

7 Test the rightness of a stand in any controversy by observing its effect on you. People who endorse the wrong side tend to be grim about it, even when they laugh. But those who support the right side usually display a certain lightness of spirit, even in their thrust to win. That is the subtle reason people will often force a laugh after they've said something unkind. They affirm a lightness that their conscience won't let them feel.

8 Devote more time to listening, if you want others to hear what *you* have to say.

9 Think, when you hear a bird singing, that its melody is expressing Nature's joy. Since you, too, are a child of Nature, you, too, can express that joy!

10 Watch yourself as if through the eyes of another. Do you like what you see? If not, make up your mind to improve. Change yourself with the same impartiality that the other person might show, were he working to change you.

11 Listen to your voice: Do you like what you hear? As the eyes are the windows of the soul, so is the voice its clear echo.

12 Relax your voice, to put warmth into it. Speak from your heart, and not thinly (as many people do), from the throat and vocal cords.

13 Look for qualities to appreciate in others. As you view them, so will you become.

14 If you find yourself becoming emotionally agitated, relax in the region of the heart. In your heart's feelings, both calmness and excitement have their beginning.

15 Live more *consciously.* Be aware of the energy flowing outward from your spine to the body. Make that flow your reality, not your bones and muscles, and you will find yourself ever filled with vitality.

16 Keep your heart open. Don't allow life to jade you. As you grow older, and lose the soft innocence which is the gift of childish ignorance—develop that refined innocence which, diamond-like, is the gift of wisdom. Keep alive in yourself the capacity for wonder.

17 Talk to give utterance to thought, and not merely to make noise.

18 Cultivate the art of brevity in words. A single well-phrased sentence will be long remembered, whereas a lengthy discourse is usually soon forgotten.

19 To express your thoughts more interestingly, infuse melody into your voice.

20 Laugh *with* others, not *at* them.

21 Choose your words kindly, and they'll invite understanding.

22 Express your thoughts simply and clearly. You do want people to understand you, don't you? Then why impose on them the burden of editing for you?

23 Think *space* when you speak. Try not to crowd your ideas.

24 Listen for people's thoughts and feelings *behind* their words.

25 Give more thought to communion with others, and communication with them will take care of itself.

26 Flow with life's changes. Don't get trapped in an abandoned time frame. The secret of aging gracefully is to greet every new experience with a fresh, creative outlook.

27 Likes and dislikes only agitate the heart's feelings. They'll prevent you from perceiving anything as it really is. Rise above them by affirming contentment regardless of any turmoil surging around you.

28 Say what you mean; mean what you say. Infuse thought and energy into every word you utter.

29 Project heart vibrations into the people with whom you are conversing, and your communication with them will be much more effective.

30 Live more fully NOW, to develop golden memories.

31 Concentrate on your present commitments. Don't dwell regretfully on failures of the past.

1 Meet your challenges vigorously. To muse lengthily on past victories is to deprive yourself of the energy you need for winning new ones.

2 Overcome worry by living bravely right now. Leave your future problems to be resolved by future energy.

3 Think of time as a radiation outward from your own center. Past and future are a circle rotating around a never-changing present.

4 Certain mental attitudes resemble postures of the body. Do you lean forward mentally, as if to grasp things before they happen? Do you lean back, as if to distance yourself from life's unpleasantness? Do you lean sideways, as if forever seeking a new strategy? Keep your mental posture upright and relaxed, and you'll find within you the power to cope with every difficulty.

5 Give old people the time to express themselves. You may find they have much wisdom to impart.

6 Your body, and not any edifice built by human hands, is your living temple. Enter the inner silence, and worship there. Send rays of devotion in solemn procession up the aisle of the spine from your heart to the high altar in the forehead, the seat of superconscious ecstasy.

7 When exercising, send energy coursing dynamically all through your body cells.

8 Be *aware* in everything you do. Let your every act be dynamic to your consciousness. To live automatically is to slip backward on your evolutionary climb toward perfect awareness.

9 Don't limit your reality to your physical body. Be conscious of space around you. Identify yourself more with non-material realities, and you'll develop increasingly the power of intuition that is latent within you.

10 Today, gaze up from time to time at the clouds. Ask them, "Have you a special message for me?" Think of consciousness as omnipresent. It is not the creation, merely, of your little brain. Reflect that the Divine can use countless instruments for our guidance and inspiration.

11 Listen to the pauses in people's speech. There, often, is where the message lies.

12 Listen with special attention to people whom you've been inclined to consider a little foolish. You may find that they, specifically, have something important to tell you. For some of our worst mistakes—which Life, for our correction, sees to it that we make—proceed from judgmental attitudes.

13 Pay more attention to children's utterances. Often, in their very lack of sophistication, they achieve the simple clarity of wisdom.

14 Live more in the heart. Send rays of love outward to all the world.

15 When you feel like lamenting anything, ask yourself, "How am I likely to feel in a week?—a month?—a year?" Sooner or later, surely, you'll stop feeling badly. So why waste all that time? Be happy now!

16 Treat others as though you were *giving* them a treat.

17 The truth never needs to be shouted, except only to make it audible to a crowd. Express your convictions calmly. Respect other people's need to arrive at the truth in their own way, and at their own pace.

18 Tell a story today to bring a smile to someone who is feeling lonely or depressed.

19 When beginning an undertaking, don't ask, "What have others done before?" Ask instead, each time, "What does this particular enterprise require?"

20 A stranger is no stranger if you can make him smile.

21 Give encouragement to a child. By doing so, you will nourish also your own high potentials.

22 You can draw strength from trees: See them as reminders of the strength in your own spine.

23 This day will belong to you, if you greet it as a friend.

24 To proclaim your opinions too loudly is to call attention to yourself, not to your ideas.

25 Treat your friends as though you still had much to learn from them.

26 Treat the world as your own, and it will always be your friend.

27 As an aid to introspection, concentrate on the rhythms of your breathing: its rate; the relative duration of inhalation to exhalation; its force; the location of its strongest flow in the nostrils; the pauses between breaths. In your breath you will find reflected every fluctuation of your heart's feelings. By watching it, your mind also will become calm.

28 Begin any discussion, where differences of opinion exist, by emphasizing points on which you and others agree. In an atmosphere of accord it is easier, usually, to settle disagreements. But in the presence of discord, even points of agreement are examined with suspicion.

29 Think of the climb up life's mountain not as a trial, but as an upward path to victory.

1 Think, when you behold a flower, that it is calling specially to *you*. Contemplate beauty in the world around you, and you yourself will become beautiful.

2 Watch little children at play: From their absorption in the moment, learn the secret of concentration.

3 Live more at the pauses between your activities.

4 Show respect for others, and they'll always respect you.

5 Be loyal to others, and they'll give you their loyalty.

6 Give others latitude to make their own mistakes. That, usually, is the only way they'll learn.

7 Expose your heart, and not only your skin, to the sun's rays. Absorb energy and joy, and you'll discover that there is another kind of solar power.

8 To expand your consciousness, concentrate on the distances in your environment.

9 Sensitize your awareness. For instance, pick up a pebble; gaze at it deeply. Does it seem to hold some special message for you? Behind its shape and coloration, sense its vibrations of energy.

10 If someone has told lies against you, respond, "You've missed the mark this time, but we agree that I'm imperfect, so—patience! A little further effort will surely give you something to talk about."

11 Speak courteously to strangers. They are your own self in different, though sometimes unexpected, forms.

12 Speak courteously to those nearest and dearest to you. For courtesy, like oil, keeps the wheels of our relationships turning smoothly.

13 What should you do if someone accuses you falsely? You might try answering, "Now that you've reduced me to a level you can handle, may we talk as friends?" The sly reprimand will be deserved!

14 Respond courteously, when people treat you discourteously. Their rudeness is not your problem. It is theirs. Courtesy, however, like a healing balm, may succeed in soothing their troubled hearts.

15 Grant other people the right to their own opinions, and you'll find yourselves in agreement on most issues.

16 Be more concerned with the *truth* of a situation, and less with how it appears to others.

17 Be more concerned with what *is* than with what you wish it were.

18 Trust Life, even if you don't feel you can trust people. Human nature is, without question, unreliable, but Life is obedient to never-changing laws.

19 Live to serve others, rather than to benefit from them. The more of yourself you can surrender in joyful service, the freer you will know yourself to be, inside.

20 Live to share with others, not to hoard for yourself, and you will be always blessed with abundance.

21 Tell your detractors, "You help me by speaking against me, for it encourages me to affirm that which alone is real to me: the joy of my inner being. Thank you, my friend. I wish you only well."

22 Laugh heartily—that is to say, from your heart—at least three times today.

23 Try to understand points of view that you don't hold. The mind, like the body, must be stretched to keep it limber. Otherwise, it will ossify.

24 When dealing with others, seek solutions that will benefit both of you. You'll find them too, then, inclined to be more generous.

25 Don't impose your ideas on anyone: *Offer* them. An idea imposed is an idea never truly accepted.

26 Life forces compromise on us. Make sure only that you adjust your compromises to your principles, and not your principles to the compromises.

27 Condemn no one. The people you oppose will work against you, never for you.

28 If counting to ten is your technique for dissipating anger, visualize each number as a progressive expansion of consciousness. An ever-broader perspective transforms anger to acceptance. Add to your expanding vision, if possible, the dimension of sympathy.

29 Don't be clever: Be sincere.

30 Today, greet a neighbor as a friend. Contradict by your good will the ancient dictum, "Your neighbor is your enemy; your neighbor's neighbor is your friend."

31 Dance more. If you can't dance physically, do so in spirit. Send joy soaring high into the sky!

1 Be generous in victory, and calmly accepting in defeat. To welcome defeat without resentment is itself a kind of victory.

2 If someone speaks of you unkindly, say to him, "Thank you. Only a friend would complain against me at the cost of his own inner peace."

3 If you have what you consider to be a good idea, welcome suggestions concerning it, but at the same time protect it, like a tender plant. Let nobody trample on your enthusiasm, like a bull loose in a field of tulips.

4 If you have a good idea, express it to friends, first, who share your ideals. Give it time to mature before exposing it to negative people who, like goats, love to gnaw on the tender shoots of other people's inspirations.

5 To attain inner freedom, mentally cast to the winds every little straw of desire and attachment.

6 Attachment is self-limiting. Visualize anything to which your feelings adhere as a prison bar, confining you. Then concentrate on the space remaining between those bars, and, into that space, make good your escape to freedom.

7 Today, tell someone to whom you feel close, "I appreciate you for what you give me."

8 Give love *today,* especially! Tell someone you feel close to, "I appreciate you for what you *are.*"

9 Let nothing tempt you to a convenient, but unethical, compromise. For where there is adherence to truth, there alone, in the end, is victory.

10 Cultivate happy memories—not in yourself only, but in others. When the opportunity comes, ask people, "What has been the best day of your life?" If their answer seems to you to fall short of their potential, continue with the question, "Why?" Draw them out, gradually, to a higher and higher understanding of what their potentials are. Convert no one, except to his own higher self.

11 When talking to people, try to tune in to their realities. Though you and they may see things very differently, communication takes place between people only when the chasm that divides them has been bridged.

12 Be more concerned with understanding others than with being understood by them, and you'll find you always have their support.

13 Be happy in yourself. To hold out your begging bowl to life, pleading for happiness, is to remain perpetually starved.

14 Hold cheerful expectations of life. Problem-consciousness can prove overwhelming. Be solution-oriented. See every problem as an *opportunity!*

15 If someone convinces you that you've committed an error, don't be upset. And don't blame yourself. Be grateful that, now, you can work to remove that impediment to your happiness. For the impediment was there, anyway. To recognize it, even belatedly, is your good fortune.

16 Welcome obstacles; see each one as a golden opportunity. If nothing else, they'll challenge you to summon up the energy in yourself to win through to victory.

17 Be restful in your heart.

18 Speak kindly to animals. To encourage them is to hasten their soul-evolution.

19 Greet everyone as a good friend.

20 Look upon members of the other sex as human beings, not as "opposites" to yourself.

21 Look upon the members of both sexes as your friends, not as antagonists on a battlefield.

22 Look upon members of the other sex as neither prey nor predators, but as brothers or sisters. As you treat them, so—far more likely—will they treat you.

23 Devote more time to serious thought. Ask yourself, "Am I doing the best I can with my life?"

24 Be decisive. Never tell yourself, merely, "I will try." Make it a declaration: "I *will!*"

25 Be practical in your expressions of friendship. Kindly sentiment, if unsupported by kind deeds, has merely sentimental value. True friendship is much more than a smile.

26 Show your appreciation to others for what they are, and for what they do. The secret of attracting abundance in life is gratitude.

27 Support others in their worthwhile goals, and let them *feel* your support. Don't merely wave at them in abstract blessing.

28 Appreciate others, and they'll give you the best that is in them.

29 Sow seeds of faith, where other have sown doubt.

30 Don't ask more of others than you would ask of yourself.

1 To develop mental clarity, be always truthful—with yourself, especially.

2 The colors of the rainbow are components of what may be called your "energy body." Develop balance in your taste for colors. Today, think *green:* green fields, green trees, the "green" of growing plants and of youthful energy!

3 Today, think *bright red:* good cheer, laughter, joy.

4 Think *blue* today: calmness, space, infinity.

5 Today, think *orange:* fiery enthusiasm to burn away all obstacles.

6 Today, think *yellow:* wisdom, understanding, calm acceptance.

7 Today, think *violet:* high thoughts, high principles, noble aspirations.

8 Think *indigo* today: pure feelings, devotion, love of beauty in all its expressions—in its spiritual expression, above all.

9 Today, think *white,* a blend of the seven colors of the rainbow: all-forgiving innocence, mental clarity, a heart kept open to the needs of others.

10 Correct others by your example, and never by nagging criticism. If you make suggestions, keep them positive. Negativity only invites more negativity.

11 When presenting an idea, clarify it with examples. The less abstract your presentation, the better it will be understood, and the more readily accepted.

12 Eat for nourishment, primarily; only secondarily for pleasure. Draw energy from the food you eat by chewing it *cheerfully,* and with concentration.

13 Happiness is not a brilliant climax to years of grim struggle and anxiety. It is a long succession of little decisions simply to *be* happy in the moment.

14 Accept adversity calmly: It is an intrinsic part of the cosmic drama. Without hardships, indeed, there would *be* no drama. But there is no adversity so great that it cannot, if accepted calmly, be turned to good advantage.

15 To balance your diet, include in it a variety of colors.

16 Make inner freedom your primary goal in life. Build a bonfire mentally, then pluck from your heart— as if from your clothing after a walk through meadow grass—every burr of attachment and desire. Cast the burrs joyfully into the flames; watch them crackle and burn away to ashes.

17 Keep your awareness centered more in the upper part of your body. Raise your energy, and your awareness will be uplifted also. When your awareness is uplifted, you'll feel happier. But when you allow your energy to sink, your consciousness becomes downcast also, and you feel unhappy.

18 With every breath you take, think that you are inhaling energy. Practice this exercise: Bend forward and exhale, then slowly raise your upper body, inhaling. Finally, stretch your hands high above the head. *Feel* the energy slowly fill your body from your toes to the very tips of your fingers.

19 Develop dynamic faith. It isn't enough merely to believe in a Higher Power, passively. Offer yourself with all the trust that is in you, that you be allowed to serve as an instrument of that Power.

20 Take the time today to *listen* to your inner silence—
and to the silence all around you, in infinity.

21 Whenever it is convenient, turn the palms of your
hands upward. You'll develop attitudes of relaxation
and acceptance.

22 Give others complete freedom to be themselves.
The more you appreciate them for what they are, the
more balanced your own outlook on life will become.

23 Don't joke too much, lest you trivialize your relationships. Friendship, especially, should be a serious commitment of the heart.

24 When giving presents to others, consider not only what they might enjoy receiving, but also what you would enjoy giving them. The greater the mutuality, the greater will be the happiness.

25 Who could ever replace any of the friends you have today? Make the most of the time you spend together.

26 *Appreciate* the differences between your ways and the ways of others. You'll soften, thereby, the hard incrustations of your mental habits.

27 Show appreciation for the opinions of others. Appreciation is the link most often missing from the chain of meaningful communication.

28 If someone criticizes you, reply, "Thank you for your suggestion. I will think about it." In that way you haven't necessarily said that you agree. All you've said is that you are keeping your mind open.

29 Forgive others, and Life itself will forgive you.

30 Accept others as they are, and you will discover friends wherever you go.

31 Nothing and no one can alter what you are in your inner self. In that interior castle, remain forever secure and at peace.

1 Accept criticism impersonally. What does it matter who offers it, or *to whom?* The issue is only one: Is the criticism valid?

2 Speak the truth impersonally, but kindly. For truth always proves beneficial, in the end.

3 Speak the truth, and Nature herself will support you in your undertakings.

4 Don't merely *look* at your environment: *Observe* it.
Be sensitive to its subtler-than-material dimensions.
Observe houses, for example. Behind their shape, style,
and color design, seek to understand their personalities.

5 Develop sensitivity as you observe things. Ask of
them, "What is your essence? What are your vibrations?" As you behold a building, ask, "What state-
ment is it making?" When you behold a garden, ask,
"What philosophy of life does it express?"

6 To heighten your awareness, consider colors as delicious beverages. Imbibe them with your heart's feeling, and you'll *know* which colors are good to keep around you, and which ones to reject.

7 Feel the wind on your skin. Ask, "Where does the wind come from? After leaving me, where will it go?" Let every breeze heighten your awareness of other places, other realities.

8 Concentrate on the taste of food—on its life force, its vitality, its joy. Have you been eating corpses? Eat only foods that are vibrant with life.

9 Don't merely *hear* sounds: *Listen* to them. Observe their effect on your nervous system. Surround yourself with uplifting harmonies, soul-stirring rhythms, inspiring melodies.

10 Make communication with others an exchange of vibrations, and not only of ideas.

11 To penetrate the confusion so often caused by words, send out tendrils, mentally, when conversing with others. Try to sense ideas even before they are expressed.

12 Study noble episodes from the lives of great men and women in history. For all of us reflect in ourselves the company we keep. Develop friends that inspire you, though your friendship span the centuries.

13 If you want to enjoy life, take yourself a little less seriously.

14 Live *in,* but not *for,* the present moment.

15 To overcome the temptation to tell tales on others, tell good ones on yourself.

16 Be good-humored about the shortcomings of others, and you'll find it easier to face your own short-comings. Remember, your faults are as overwhelming or as insignificant as your own imagination makes them.

17 Give others credit, where possible, in the anecdotes you tell.

18 To live simply is to breathe the air of true freedom. Don't suffocate in the stale-aired closet of useless possessions!

19 Look for the larger purpose beyond every undertaking, and for the greater reality of which every thing is a part.

20 In the colors you select, whether in your clothing or your environment, bring harmony to your life, not dissonance.

21 To develop concentration, do one thing at a time, and do it well.

22 To develop will power, focus your energies. In what way do people scatter them? By doing things half-heartedly.

23 What do you want from others: love? support? loyalty? Whatever it is, give that first to them.

24 Be supportive of other people's enthusiasms. To belittle them is only to betray one's own selfishness and egotism.

25 Before speaking, weigh your words—but not *too* heavily.

26 Be willing, when occasion permits, to give others the last word.

27 Eat light foods more frequently than heavy ones. Drink at least two quarts of liquid a day. The lighter your food, the lighter also will be your consciousness.

28 When out walking, be aware that the energy of the universe is manifested in your body. The more conscious you become of that energy, the more inexhaustible your supply of it will be.

29 If possible, be certain that you'll do a thing before you promise to do it. Be true to your word, always.

30 Accept criticism impartially. Remember, truth is, in all things, the final arbiter.

1 When you find yourself in a crowd, hold the thought: "All these people are my brothers and sisters." Emanate love and harmony from your heart. Any disharmony in your surroundings, then, will not be able to affect you.

2 Don't *drive* the people working under you: *Inspire* them.

3 Laugh at other people's jokes as though you'd be delighted to have told them yourself.

4 Make your happiness unconditional, by emphasizing its independence of anything outside yourself.

5 Train yourself—your heart as well as your mind—to say YES to life!

6 Encourage good ideas, no matter what their source.

7 Go out of your way to show respect and kindness to people whom others have ignored.

8 Calm the feelings of your heart. Without inner peace, there can be no happiness.

9 If you can forgive someone toward whom you've held a grudge, you will catch at least a glimpse of what it means to be truly free.

10 Make everyone you meet feel that he or she is in some way special to you. Don't particularize that specialness, necessarily. Project, rather, the sense of specialness you feel in yourself, as a child of Infinity.

11 Make contentment your criterion of prosperity. Wealth is the *consciousness* of abundance, primarily. And poverty is the *consciousness* of lack. Be ever comfortable within your means.

12 Watch the birds fly. Visually, there isn't anything to keep them aloft, and yet—they fly. There's a power that sustains you, too, though you can't see it. Today, have the faith to try your wings.

13 Be expansive in your sympathies. Don't limit them to thoughts of "I" and "mine."

14 Visualize yourself as a surfer, riding the waves of opportunity. Select the wave you like best, then see how far it will take you. To accomplish anything worthwhile in your life, unite your energy to that of a Greater Power.

15 Opportunity is no accident. It must be attracted. Seek it with confident, cheerful expectation, and it will find you even on a crowded street.

16 See no one as a stranger. The sorrows and joys of humanity are all much like your own.

17 When you decide to do something, back it with the full power of your will. Your mental development depends far more on the *quality* of energy you put out than on any thing you do, specifically.

18 Most of the pains we experience, mentally as well as physically, are painful only because we so define them. Think of them as sensations, merely, or events, and you'll find that you can bear them relatively easily.

19 Regardless of how people treat you, determine your response by the criterion of inner freedom. How they behave is their business; how *you* respond is your own. Supposing, then, that someone expresses hatred for you. Don't you *know* that you feel freer when you give love?

20 Is there any subject on which you are too sensitive? If so, take a good look at yourself. Ask, "What am I protecting in myself? *And why?*"

21 Rest or move surrounded by the aura created by your inner peace. Others will be drawn into it even if they've been at war.

22 Be more encouraging of others, and less critical. By too much criticism you'll stifle their creativity and paralyze your own.

23 To overcome a judgmental tendency in yourself, observe others who are themselves afflicted with that tendency. They judge because they are distrustful of others as well as of themselves. And what they distrust most of all is originality. Their first question in any situation is, "What is proper? What is done?" Their vision is narrow because the route they travel is a rut.

24 Be open to others—to their projects, their ideas. Thus, their interests will balance and enrich your own.

25 Explore the relationships, more than the differences, between other people's ideas and your own.

26 Meet anger silently, but with respect, and its fires will subside for lack of fuel.

27 Defuse criticism by saying, "Thank you. I appreciate knowing how you feel. Please let me think it over."

28 Defuse criticism by saying, "Let's be friends, even if we don't agree on everything."

29 Disarm critics by saying to them, "I see and appreciate your point of view. Now, may I offer an alternative?"

30 If possible, defuse criticism by saying, "I agree with you. Let's see if, together, we can't find a practical solution."

31 The world mirrors back to you either your wisdom or your folly. If you see anything in others that displeases you, ask yourself, "How can I change myself?"

1 Today, take special note of other people's virtues. See whether your awareness doesn't draw out the best in them, and encourage those same virtues in yourself.

2 Encourage people in their strengths, and never belittle them for their weaknesses. By giving strength to others, you yourself will grow stronger. But in demeaning others you will only demean yourself. The color you paint a fence is the color you get on your own hands.

3 Work at developing your strengths—at fighting battles against your lower self that you have a chance of winning. When you are strong enough to banish a weakness, do so forcefully. But don't struggle ineffectually against flaws that are too deep-seated. The stronger you become in yourself, the easier it will be for you to banish all shortcomings.

4 Whenever possible, invite participation in the decisions you make. Bear in mind, however, this simple fact: If a decision is yours to make, the responsibility for it is yours also. Allow no one's suggestions to become your excuse for failure. Accept only those ideas which resonate with your inner feelings.

5 Enlist support for your ideas, but remember, "Yes-man" support is a blindfold, not an aid.

6 Wherever possible, give credit to others—even, sometimes, when an idea was first your own.

7 Develop straightforwardness in your gaze. When speaking with others, don't talk to the floor, nor gaze long and earnestly at the wall. Look at them directly. You'll find it easier to develop clarity in your own thinking.

8 What is the best handshake? Firm, as an expression of honest friendship. Don't make it so firm, however, that you appear aggressive.

9 Make it a practice, when you converse with some-one, to look at him or her between the eyebrows, and not only in the eyes. To stare too fixedly into the eyes may seem an invasion of privacy. If you look away, people may think you have donned a mask. To shift your gaze back and forth constantly from one eye to the other conveys an impression of restlessness. Let your gaze be calm and centered. You'll draw the other person to a center, also.

10 Be aware of the tone of your voice. Infuse it with kindness by speaking more from the heart, and with will power and determination by projecting your vocal tone out through the forehead. Note how instantly the human voice expresses anger, self-interest, or indifference. Project tones of kindness, and you'll find it more natural to *be* kind.

11 Listen to melodies that have an uplifting influence. For some melodies fill the heart with happiness, whereas others fill it with sorrow. Shun as poison any melody that makes the heart restless or negative. Music, more than any other art form, penetrates the mind and affects it from within.

12 The quality of your speech can tell you much about yourself. Listen to it sensitively. Do you speak with a nasal tone? That may indicate a tendency to look down your nose at others. Try to be less certain that you alone know best. Or, again, do you place a heavy emphasis on vowels? Ask yourself in that case, "Could I be helped by being less emotional?"

13 Listen to the sounds of your speech. Do you find yourself placing a strong emphasis on consonants? If so, consider whether you need greater sensitivity in your dealings with others.

14 Listen to the sounds of your speech. Do you find yourself speaking in a monotone? If so, develop more enthusiasm, by expressing it in your voice. Become interested in sharing your ideas. To magnetize your voice and make it more interesting, practice speaking for a few minutes every day in a higher register—in a falsetto range, if possible.

15 Listen to the melody of your speech. Let it express what you sincerely feel in your heart. Shun melodies that are merely the product of social conditioning.

16 Face your trials cheerfully; don't shrink from them. For trials are like dogs: They lose heart when we confront them, but give eager chase the moment we turn and flee.

17 There will never be another today. Make the most of it.

18 Offer suggestions to help others, and not simply as a purgative for your own negative emotions. Above all, never undermine a person's faith in himself.

19 Laugh with your whole being, not only with your vocal cords.

20 Be calm even when the hurricanes of trials lash you. No calamity can shake you, if you develop calmness at your inner center.

21 Seek the approval of people whose opinions you respect. The applause of multitudes is like ocean surf: effervescent, and at the same time evanescent. Better the scolding of the wise than the adulation of fools.

22 Give credit to others for the things you've accomplished together.

23 Look at a river, or imagine one: Think of it as expressing the flow of your own thoughts. Affirm silently: "I adapt like flowing water to new situations and ideas."

24 Think of something that you fear to lose, then ask yourself, "Were I to lose it, would I be a different person than I am today?" In yourself, be contented. Be whole.

25 Think of things to which you feel emotionally attached, then toss them into the air like flower petals. Watch them float away on the wind, diminishing with distance until they disappear. Affirm joyously, "In my heart, forever, I am free!"

26 Devote less time to passive entertainment, such as watching television, and more to understanding things for yourself. Passivity is to creativity what floating on water is to swimming.

27 Communicate with others thoughtfully, never absentmindedly. Do things that are uplifting; don't merely pass the time. For time is an inheritance: However little or much has been allotted to you, spend it wisely, or it will be frittered away.

28 Be silent at your center. Excessive speech is anesthetizing. Instead of thinking up ideas to communicate to others, think up ideas to communicate to your own higher self.

29 Accommodate your ideas to the good suggestions of others. What does the source of an idea really matter? The more closely the idea approaches to the truth, the less credit anyone ought to claim for it. For where we human beings intrude on the process, usually, is in our mistakes.

30 Make a special effort today to break out of your self-enclosures, whether of selfishness, or timidity, or self-preoccupation. Expand your awareness to include the needs of other people.

31 In your enjoyment of things, observe your mental process. Let nothing possess you: Be ever self-possessed.

1 Remain always even-minded and cheerful. To rise and fall with the waves of emotion is to sacrifice mental clarity for confusion.

2 View your problems dispassionately, as if from a mountain peak. Perspective is lost in the narrow valley of personal involvement.

3 Rise above your likes and dislikes, but don't withhold sympathy from others. Too many people reverse these priorities: They soar loftily above the likes and dislikes of others, but are tenderly sympathetic where their own interests are involved.

4 Non-attachment is not indifference. Be deeply concerned with finding solutions to people's problems.

5 Walk tall, physically and also mentally. Keep your spine straight, and your thinking straightforward. Wisdom is spherical, but the path to victory is linear.

6 As a gardener waters the flowers, so water the hearts of others.

7 Offer hope to those who are losing hope. Help them to see that their potentials reach out to infinity.

8 Offer encouragement, wherever you find sorrow or despair. No defeat is permanent; often, it is the precursor to stunning victory.

9 Offer happiness, wherever you see gloom. Pity is demeaning, but happiness, offered without imposing it, can be a lifeboat on a stormy sea.

10 Put bright colors in your surroundings, and you'll bring more brightness and color to your own life.

11 Be as considerate of the feelings of others as you would have them be of your own.

12 Be courageous in your decision making. "What if?" and "What if not?" keep people sitting forever on a fence. Even a poor decision may be preferable to making no decision at all: At least it will keep the energy flowing, a flow which may, in time, attract good decisions.

13 Be modest, but don't belittle yourself. The center of your being is the center of the universe as far as your own understanding is concerned. At that center, awaiting your discovery, lies all the power of Infinity.

14 Misfortune lies in our perception of things, not in the things themselves. Never complain, no matter what you have to endure. Whining merely tests other people's patience. But courage in the face of adversity wins universal admiration.

15 Accept your lot in life cheerfully, no matter how difficult it seems. Yours is what you've attracted to yourself, and therefore earned; it is your own special pathway to enlightenment.

16 In life's race, compete against yourself, primarily. Don't be too concerned with how well other people run. That athlete runs best who looks straight ahead. That athlete wins the most who improves on his own record.

17 How valuable, really, is other people's admiration? You aren't central in their lives. Much of the praise they heap on you today they may retract tomorrow. Seek to shine brightly before your own conscience.

18 To do a thing well, concentrate on every detail while at the same time exerting the will to keep your full purpose always in mind. This constant tuning of the details to your underlying purpose is one of the secrets of genius. Another is to draw on Higher Consciousness for your inspiration, and not to depend on the vagaries of human intelligence. There is no such thing as a genius quotient of intelligence.

19 Don't "gobble" the future. Do one thing at a time, carefully and with full absorption. Time will stop for you, if you do. And, with time's suspension, you will gain a taste of bliss in your soul.

20 Look to the past as a guideline to improving the future, but seek perfection beyond time, in the eternal NOW.

21 When troubles beset you, seek their cause, and their solution, at their true source in yourself. Never accept for yourself the victim's role.

22 Do you reject the thought of God? If so, try thinking of Him, or Her, as the highest potential you can imagine for yourself. Don't you see? There is a need in human nature for high aspiration. "Survival of the fittest" doesn't do it for us. Why *not*, indeed, love God?

23 Seek freedom within yourself. Soul-freedom is your one and only "inalienable right."

24 You have within you the power to overcome all adversity. Concentrate, today, on living by that inner power.

25 In yourself lies the only key to happiness there is. Think of the things, the people, the circumstances with which you've identified your happiness, and visualize them as colors of the rainbow, brilliant in the sunlight of your eager expectations, but in themselves raindrops, merely, with no color of their own.

26 Adopt a serviceful attitude. Far from demeaning you, it will expand your self-identity, and will greatly increase your stature before others—not those, perhaps, who are steeped in worldly pride, but all those gifted with sensitivity and understanding.

27 Welcome challenge, and it will work with you, not against you.

28 If moods oppress you, offer them into broader perceptions of reality. Moods are the dark effluence squeezed out of the heart by our contractive feelings. Expand your feelings, and your moods will evaporate, to vanish in cloudless skies of inner freedom.

29 Burn away your moods by the blazing power of your will, concentrated fiercely at the forehead between the eyebrows—the seat of higher consciousness in the body.

30 Uplift moods of depression on wings of song—or, if you are not musically gifted, soar upward mentally with the flights of birds. Moods come to us because our energy has descended to the lower part of our bodies. When we raise our level of energy, the moods vanish for lack of native air to breathe.

1 Be more concerned with entertaining kind feelings toward others than with what their feelings may be toward you. Whatever those feelings, you'll be happier in yourself for expressing kindness.

2 Love people—if not for themselves, then for the pure joy of loving.

3 If you feel impelled to defend a principle, make joy the heart of your defense. Fight to win, never to injure or destroy.

4 Wrap yourself in a cloak of calmness. A strong, calm will, wisely guided, will be your best protection against adversity.

5 Use discrimination like a sword: With its sharp blade, slice in two the dilemmas life places before you. Separate right from wrong, truth from error, and charity from unfeeling insistence on precedent, or on "the principle of the thing."

6 If you fight for the truth, and resolutely renounce self-interest, you *cannot but* win, in the end.

7 Rid yourself of all self-definitions, such as "liberal" or "conservative." Are you a Christian? Fine. But realize, at the same time, that there are as many types of Christianity as there are Christians; as many types of Judaism as there are Jews; as many types of atheism, even, as there are atheists. Be yourself, simply: unique among all human beings.

8 When working with others, remember this simple axiom: "People are more important than things."

9 Hold cheerful expectations of life. Your magnetic field will attract whatever resonates with itself. The quality of energy you put out, therefore, determines what you'll receive in return.

10 Reach out in sympathy to others; don't wait for them first to reach out to you. For there are many wounded on life's battlefield. People protect their feelings for fear of being stabbed again. Be a spiritual medic, ready to help those who are in psychological pain. Don't wait for their appreciation in return.

11 Face the world courageously. You are a child of God, and, as such, the equal of anyone on earth. Your potential for greatness is your eternal truth; your shortcomings are your merely temporary delusions. A painting should be judged in its finished state, not from the artist's mistakes while his work is still in progress.

12 Stand courageously by the lessons you've learned in life. No matter how popular a cause, be ruled by what *you* know, not by what others claim to know. If compromise is necessary, in the name of harmony, let no concession to others lessen your faith in the lessons learned from your own experience. To surrender the castle is a very different thing from inviting people to enter it as guests.

13 Give others their due, and with that same generosity allow others to give you yours, also. To reject sincere praise is to impugn the good taste of the person offering it.

14 Be humble, but never be abject. True humility is not self-abasement: It is self-forgetfulness in the contemplation of broader realities. In bright sunlight, why apologize for the light of your candle? The important thing is that, in sunlight, everyone can see.

15 Be dignified, but not proud. Develop an awareness of the divine power within you to accomplish all things.

16 Be matter-of-fact about your own accomplishments, but proud of the accomplishments of others. To expand your sense of ego is one of the best ways of transcending it.

17 To develop your powers of memory, concentrate one-pointedly on everything you do. To develop the power of soul-memory, concentrate on the things you do, but without attachment. Knowledge depends on the power of memory, but wisdom comes with soul-memory.

18 Concentration is, in everything, the key to success. To penetrate ice, push upon it with a sharp point. To overcome the obstacles in your life, bring your mental energy similarly to a point, and tunnel through them.

19 Possess things, as necessary, but let no thing possess you.

20 Don't close your heart, when your feelings have been hurt. For contraction causes its own pain. How others behave toward you is like the weather: not under your control. But how *you* behave, and what your feelings are, need be determined by no one but yourself. To accept a hurt from anyone is to suffer twice.

21 The cure for a broken heart is not to stop loving: It is to love more wholeheartedly. True love is not infatuation, and is therefore not rooted in selfish desire. Separate your heart's feelings from all dependence on externals.

22 Wish the best for everybody, and, in the very act of blessing them, you yourself will be blessed. A stained-glass window, with the sunlight pouring through it, is even brighter and more beautiful than the light with which it graces a church.

23 Be not afraid to love. Even if your love is unrequited, *you* will be the richer for having loved. Water that doesn't flow grows stagnant.

24 Be sensitive to Nature's moods—not to subject yourself to them, but to keep yourself open to sources of inspiration outside your little ego.

25 Dare to dream greatness. Without courage, the doors of scientific discovery would have remained locked; the wilderness would have continued to seem hostile; and the poet would never have left his rustic village.

26 Be a student, not a teacher. Even if you find yourself in the role of teacher, remain a student still, sharing with your friends, simply, fresh insights and discoveries.

27 If you see anything you dislike, in others or in the world, consider first whether it is *you* who need changing. The appearance of wrong may be improved by changing one's outlook. People once thought the night came because the sun had left them. And then it was discovered that the night came because the earth had turned.

28 Concentrate on winning your present battles, and the course of the war will take care of itself. At the same time, never sacrifice your integrity to your desire to win. Cling to principle with that devotion which armies once showed in the defense of their flag.

29 To overcome anger, reflect that today's mood may well be transformed into tomorrow's laughter. The same energy would be merely redirected. Why not, then, redirect your energy toward laughter even *now?*

30 Overcome anger by reflecting on the great number of views that are held on almost every subject. Calmness manifests itself at the rest point between two alternatives. Relax mentally at that point. In calmness ask yourself, "Am I indeed omniscient? Is my view alone infallible?"

31 To overcome anger, attach greater importance to harboring feelings of good will.

1 Keep a sense of humor, especially when things don't turn out as you hoped. For life is a play—indeed, a tragi-comedy. To cope with disappointment, look ahead to future scenes that will surely offer comic relief. Be an observer of life, and less intensely involved as a participant.

2 Try always to maintain a sense of humor. Don't bludgeon others with it, however, if you find them unreceptive. Along with your sense of humor, be *good* humored, and kind.

3 Before making any important decision in life, consult your inner silence. There, awaiting you as if in a deep forest, lies the wellspring of spiritual insight.

4 Develop gracefulness of movement. Awkward or jerky movements induce, as well as reflect, disconnected thinking, but gracefulness will bring a smoother flow to your thoughts.

5 Have the courage to embrace the unexpected. For life is an unfolding drama. Whatever happens to you, welcome it with a smile and you'll find you can turn it to good advantage.

6 In any position of leadership, inspire others by your example. What you *do* has more influence than anything you *say*. And what you *are* has a greater influence than either.

7 Be circumspect in both action and speech. Don't expose yourself unnecessarily to people's misunderstanding and foolish criticism.

8 Accept praise good-humoredly. Reflect that what you receive today may be withdrawn tomorrow, and that even praise well-earned can become a yoke upon your neck if you take it too seriously. Be ruled by your own conscience, not by the opinions of others. Praise and blame, very often, are the opposite sides of a single, counterfeit coin.

9 Give praise sincerely, but never flatter anyone. Sincere praise can inspire others to great heights, but flattery will only lull them with the suggestion, "You've done so much already! Why put yourself out to climb any higher?"

10 Judge no one. For who knows what hardships others have endured? In their mistakes they demonstrate their kinship with us all.

11 Judge no one, and you will be kindly judged by all people of good will. The judgment of people of ill will, on the other hand, deserves no hearing outside of the confessional.

12 Why compare yourself with others, whether to your detriment or your advantage? When you are driving on the freeway, many cars are ahead of you, and quite as many behind. Keep your mind focused serenely on your own destination.

13 Dress to give pleasure—to others, and also to your-self—but don't dress merely to show off. To give plea-sure is self-expansive, but to vie for others' admiration will only produce in you a contractive consciousness.

14 Be a healing influence. Light, and not a preoccupa-tion with darkness, is the antidote to darkness. Seek solutions: Don't concentrate on problems. Promote goodness: Don't be a knight errant, seeking out and destroying evil. Bring joy to people's lives: Don't sacri-fice your happiness to eliminate their suffering.

15 A person's magnetism is an expression of his consciousness. Improve your magnetism by infusing everything you do with positive thoughts and energy. The more joyful and loving your consciousness, the more uplifting will be your magnetism.

16 Today, be a peace-maker: not in the sense of reconciling differences, but of emanating inner peace to all. Harmonize the vibrations of your heart; then expand those vibrations into your environment and into the hearts of all with whom you come in contact.

17 Be aware of the inevitability of feeling's influence on reason. To suppress your feelings would be merely to distort their influence on your intellect. But to refine feeling into calm intuition—that is the secret for guiding reason surely to the truth.

18 Think of life as a ski run, not as a game of chess in which every move is carefully plotted in advance. For there should be a flow in life, a flow that reasoned analysis often only disturbs.

19 Treat others as colleagues, not as competitors. Competition can be an incentive to self-improvement, but it takes cooperation to build a civilization. When people work together, they benefit everyone. A thousand streams, meeting, become a mighty river.

20 Be truthful always, and you'll develop the power to make things happen simply because you decreed them.

21 We are all actors on the stage of life. To act your part well, listen for the Director's inner guidance. Heed it, and you'll find happiness and inner freedom; ignore it, and you'll find alienation—from the world, from other people, and—worst of all—from your own self.

22 To develop courage, hold your chest up as if breasting a wave. Physical posture reflects mental attitudes. Adopt postures that will reinforce qualities that you want to develop in yourself.

23 Listen everywhere for the voice of good counsel. If you hold yourself truly open, you may hear it even in the wind.

24 Take time to listen to the children playing. From their laughter, learn lessons in innocence. From their openness, learn lessons in trust. From their guileless-ness, learn lessons in truthfulness and sincerity. It isn't maturity that robs us of these virtues: It is immaturity, embittered by disappointment. With maturity comes understanding; from understanding comes acceptance; and from acceptance, finally, comes wisdom.

25 Be less concerned to express yourself cleverly than to express what is true. For cleverness is like stylish clothing: useless, if it covers a corpse.

26 Gain wisdom from experience; don't seek it from books. What you read will never be wholly yours until you've lived it.

27 Develop loyalty—to your family, your friends, your chosen path in life. Loyalty, like a rudder, will hold your ship true to its course. Be loyal above all to the truth as you yourself best understand it.

28 No one else, ever, will be as good at being *you* as you are. Be true to yourself, to your understanding, to your ideals. Your contribution to humanity, then, will be unique and valuable.

29 Make creativity a philosophy of life—not originality, in the sense of being different, but creative originality in the sense of developing perceptivity from within. The first step to creativity is perceptive imitation of excellence. The second is to view each situation as unique and as requiring, therefore, perceptive handling. The third is to draw from that situation some hidden truth, as you yourself are best able to perceive it.

30 Seek, in recreation, to *re-create* yourself. During the pauses between activities, seek that *inner* pause where creativity is renewed. Withdraw to your temple of inner silence and, there, focus and re-energize your thoughts.

1 Hold expectations of success, but don't let expectation take the place of painstaking effort. People who brag about what they are going to accomplish overlook, all too often, the little steppingstones of details that everyone must cross to achieve success.

2 Do things, not for applause, but for the far more satisfying approval of your conscience.

3 Do your best; then leave the consequences to work themselves out. Attachment to results only diminishes the ability to work effectively in the present. But with non-attachment, if success in one endeavor proves a shimmering mirage, your energy will remain free to try again, and ever yet again.

4 Whenever you see colors that you like especially, absorb them into yourself; let them vitalize your aura. Liking for a particular color may suggest a need for it, as the craving for a particular food may indicate elements that are lacking in one's diet.

5 Practice patience. For patience is the straightest and smoothest highway to success.

6 Show respect for convention, but remember that conventions were first created by unconventional people.

7 Don't think, "How can I do this differently?" Don't even think, "How can I do it better?" Think, "What is the *right* way to do it?"

8 Others may see you as their enemy: Resolve, for your part, to be their friend.

9 To attract abundance, see money as a flow of energy, not as a static quantity. See life as a flow also, not as a fixed pattern. Think of life as a glass, and of abundance as a flow of water. Water can fill the glass only in liquid form, not as a block of ice.

10 In any effort to improve your life, work first on improving yourself. To depend on others' good treatment of you is a slave's attitude. Become a cause in your life, not an effect. *Self*-dependence is the mark of heroism.

11 Include success for others in your dreams for your own success. Better a stream that irrigates a green valley than a desert oasis, surrounded by vast stretches of sand.

12 Attachment is like an unripe fruit, which clings to the tree even when buffeted by winds. Be like the ripe fruit, which falls without effort at the first touch of a breeze.

13 A true friend is one with whom you can weep, not one with whom you only laugh. Weep with others in their sorrows. But never weep for yourself.

14 Think vastness! Think eternity! Don't limit yourself to your little body and its fleeting needs. Your very thoughts are but waves on the ocean of Infinite Consciousness.

15 Love others as aspects of your own Self. Every human being specializes on your behalf, and on behalf of the human race, in developing a unique expression of potentials that are universal.

16 Don't compare others' fortunes to your own. Rejoice with them in their successes, which have been earned by them. Your own, too, will be uniquely yours: They can belong to no one else.

17 Hold good will in your heart for all mankind. For we are all travelers in a vast desert, struggling to reach the sea. We need one another's cooperation, and friendship, and support—lest in the heat of travel our strength be exhausted, and we collapse alone on the sand.

18 As you wash your body, so wash your heart daily of the impurities of attachment and desire.

19 Imagine your attachments soaring like balloons high into the sky. Watch them vanish into the distance. Then return your mind's focus to your own heart; enjoy, there, the feeling of relief and inner freedom.

20 As you begin this day, tell yourself, "Today I am incarnated anew! I am released from the hypnosis of my old habits and mistakes! Everything that I have long dreamed of doing I *will* accomplish in this, my new life."

21 Be confident—not of your own powers, but of God's. Never boast. All that you have and are is yours only on loan.

22 Give up thinking, "This is mine! all mine!" Tell God, "All this is Thine! only Thine!"

23 Understand originality to be, not something that no one has ever done before, but something that originates in you. Though it have been expressed by others a thousand times, your own sincere expression of it will make it uniquely yours.

24 To be creative, relax first, mentally. Let creativity become a flow of intuition passing through you.

25 The gift of kind words is more precious than any present bought, then wrapped in cheery token, only, of your friendship.

26 Every truly creative act is conceived uniquely in eternity. Whenever you accomplish something, erase the thought of it from your mind, that your next accomplishment express its own uniqueness.

27 Direct energy into everything you do. For energy has its own intelligence. It will make things happen for you that you could never plan.

28 Develop a sense of community with others. This community should consist of more than your family, more than the town or city in which you live, more than your own country. Expand your awareness of community to include the entire world.

29 Simplify your way of looking at things. Complexity of thought only brings complexity to your work, your relationships, your entire life.

30 Respect excellence wherever you encounter it. True excellence is neither enhanced nor diminished by the name of its achiever. It is a reality in itself, impersonal, as universal as the air.

31 Don't wait until tomorrow to scale the mountain of your dreams. *Do it NOW!*

Selected Other Books By J. Donald Walters:

The "Secrets" series — a thought for every day of the month:

Secrets of Happiness
Secrets of Love
Secrets of Friendship
Secrets of Inner Peace
Secrets of Success
Secrets for Men
Secrets for Women
Secrets of Prosperity

Secrets of Leadership
Secrets of Self-Acceptance
Secrets of Winning People
Secrets of Radiant Health and
Well-Being
Secrets of Emotional Healing
Secrets of Bringing Peace on Earth

The Art of Supportive Leadership — a practical handbook for people in positions of responsibility, one that views leadership in terms of shared accomplishments rather than of personal advancement.

Money Magnetism — use money as a vehicle for higher awareness. Learn how to attract whatever you need in life, when you need it.

Affirmations for Self-Healing — an inspiring discussion of fifty-two spiritual qualities, with an affirmation and prayer for the realization of each one